What Blointer

Other Books by Maria Mazziotti Gillan

Flowers from the Tree of Night, Chantry Press, 1980
Winter Light, Chantry Press, 1985
Luce D'Inverno, Cross-Cultural Communications, 1987
The Weather of Old Seasons, Cross-Cultural Communications, 1987
Taking Back My Name, Malafemmina Press, 1990; Lincoln Springs Press,
    1991, repeated printings
Where I Come From: Selected and New Poems, Guernica Editions, 1995, 1997
Things My Mother Told Me, Guernica Editions, 1999
Italian Women in Black Dresses, Guernica Editions, 2002, 2003, 2004
Maria Mazziotti Gillan: Greatest Hits 1972-2002,
    Pudding House Publications, 2003
Talismans/Talismani, Ibiskos Editions, 2006
All That Lies Between Us, Guernica Editions, 2007
Nightwatch, Poems by Maria Mazziotti and Aeronwy Thomas,
    The Seventh Quarry Press, 2010
Moments in the Past That Shine, The Ridgeway Press, 2010
What We Pass On: Collected Poems: 1980-2009, Guernica Editions, 2010
The Place I Call Home, NYQ Books, 2012
Writing Poetry to Save Your Life: How to Find the Courage to Tell Your Stories,
    MiroLand, Guernica, 2013
The Silence in an Empty House, NYQ Books, 2013
Ancestors' Song, Bordighera Press, 2013
The Girls in the Chartreuse Jackets, Cat in the Sun Books, 2014
In a Place of Flowers and Light: San Mauro and Mia Mama,
    a cura di Osvaldo Marrocco, 2014
*Women Who Are Afraid of Nothing: Storia Del Passato Perduto E Mai Piu
    Ritrovato,* a cura di Osvaldo Marrocco, translated from English to Italian
    by Maria Giovanna Barra, 2016

What Blooms in Winter

Maria Mazziotti Gillan

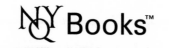

Books™

The New York Quarterly Foundation, Inc.
New York, New York

NYQ Books™ is an imprint of The New York Quarterly Foundation, Inc.

The New York Quarterly Foundation, Inc.
P. O. Box 2015
Old Chelsea Station
New York, NY 10113

www.nyq.org

First Edition

Set in New Baskerville

Layout and Design by Raymond P. Hammond

Cover illustration by Maria Mazziotti Gillan

Photograph of author provided by Joseph Costa | www.LaModaStudio.com

Library of Congress Control Number: 2016933809

ISBN: 978-1-63045-011-3

What Blooms in Winter

Acknowledgments

Grateful acknowledgments to the editors of the following journals in which these poems, sometimes in early versions, first appeared or are forthcoming: "Why I Loved the Library," "Our First TV," and "My Sister Was the One," *Lips,* 2015; "Bookbags and Galoshes," "Miss Cherry," and "It's My Gillan Pot Roast," *Lips,* 2016; "The First Day of High School" and "My Mother Was a Brilliant Cook," *Voices in Italian Americana,* 2016; "The Clothes I Wore in High School," *Narrative Northeast,* issue #3, 2015; "At the Factory Where My Mother Worked," *The Wide Shore: A Journal of Global Women's Poetry,* issue #3, 2015; "Trading in the VW Bus" and "What I Can't Tell My Son," *San Diego Poetry Annual,* 2016-2017; "Under the Grape Arbor," *Narrative Northeast,* issue #4, 2016; "First Communion Photo," "Be a Human Fly," and "Italian Summer," Ishka Bibble, 2016; "The Day I Lost My Daughter in Macy's" and "What Blooms in Winter," *San Diego Poetry Annual,* 2015-2016; "How Many Hours," *Mom Egg Review,* volume 13, 2015; "I Tell People I've Let You Go" and "My Daughter at 2," *Louisiana Literature,* volume 34 #1, 2016; "The Signer at Nelson Mandela's Funeral," *MiPoesias* online, March 2015; "This Is How Memory Works," *When Women Waken—Delight,* 2014; "What the Body Knows," *Prairie Schooner,* volume 81 #4, winter 2007; "Grief," *Tiferet,* Autumn 2015; "Oak Place, Hawthorne, NJ," *Tiferet,* Autumn 2016; "Today the Forsythia," *Big Scream,* #54, 2013-2015, Sacred Lands & Waters issue in memory of Jeff Poniewaz; "In Sicily," *Arba Sicula,* translated into Italian by Gaetano Cipolla, Fall 2014; "It's been a week," *Rattle,* December, #50, 2015.

With gratitude to Susan Amsterdam, Susan Lembo Balik, Clara M. Barnhart, Linda Hillringhouse, and Joe Weil for their assistance in editing and proofing this book.

for Susan Lembo Balik,
in gratitude for her careful editing and proofing of this book

Contents

I. Bookbags and Galoshes

II. All We Didn't Know

III. A Season of Loss

I. Bookbags and Galoshes

Seventeenth Street in Paterson, NJ

1.
Why is it in memory that I always visit
the street where I grew up, 17th Street
with its two- and three-family houses,
its bar and candy store,
its vacant lot filled with wildflowers.
When the Ivy League reporters take me there
to interview me and take pictures, I can tell
they are horrified—the garbage in the street,
the discarded liquor bottles,
the vacant lot no longer vacant,
but filled with a rectangle
of ugly garages. I know they don't see
the street the way I did,
lit by memory, the time between then and now
has already erased anything ugly or cruel about that street.
In memory, it is always summer. I have been playing
in the street—tag or hide-and-seek or hopscotch.
At dusk, we try to hang onto these last moments
before our mothers' voices call us home
for supper. One by one, we walk to our back doors.
Through the screen, I see my mother placing bowls of food
on the oilcloth-covered table. Inside, she will pour me
a glass of milk from the bottle the milkman delivers
to the backdoor each day, and we will sit together
eating and talking. After supper, we'll play games,
like Monopoly or gin rummy or maybe my mother
will have us wash up and change out of our play clothes,
and we'll walk together up 4th Avenue
to 25th Street to visit my Zia Rosa and Zio Gianni,
where other people from Riverside,
my honorary aunts and cousins, would also arrive.
Later we'd walk home together in the summer dark.

How can I explain to these two young people
with their degrees from Harvard and Yale
how happy I was then, how happy
to have these memories to carry
like a shimmery light in my hands?

2.
Every day in summer, we'd go outside—down the step
from the back porch, down the walk that hugged the side
of the two-family house where we lived on 17th Street
in Paterson, NJ—and soon a throng of other kids would join us,
coming from the other houses on the street. Often we'd play
in the vacant lot overgrown with tall weeds and black-eyed Susans
and daisies, the days stretching out before us
as we played hide-and-seek and tag, the air heavy
with the aroma of grass and flowers. We had
crepe paper whirlers that we twirled around our heads
and we'd move out to the sidewalk and play hopscotch,
and hit the street for games of stickball. We wouldn't
go home again until our mothers called us in for lunch, and then
back out again into the hazy summer afternoons. After supper, we
would sit together on our back stoop and whisper to one another.
We smoked punks to keep away mosquitoes, and the next day, we'd
repeat what we had done the day before, never tiring of each other
or the games we played, the world to us so new, so rich for exploration,
July and August so full, we were sure they'd never end.
We could not imagine a time when those summers wouldn't shine in
our memories. Today, our grandchildren go on play dates
or stay home alone, playing on their computers,
the streets around their large houses empty, no sounds
of children playing at dusk, no one outside at all, and I know that
all the expensive games and toys cannot make up
for one hour of those long ago summers.
How perfect those days, how fortunate we are,
to carry them inside us like treasures.

We Used to Call It Downtown, Remember?

We used to call it downtown, remember? When we
were still young, and we'd hop the bus downtown
and walk up Main Street to Meyer Brothers
and wander the perfume aisles. The elevator
to the second floor was guarded
by the white-gloved operator who would say,
"Step to the back of the car please. Second floor."
Then she'd announce what was sold there—
dresses and sweaters, and up
to the third floor, towels and rugs.

We never bought anything, but we liked to look, finger
the silk lingerie, feel the soft mohair sweaters, then
we'd go out through the revolving door to the bustle
of the street and browse through Quackenbush's
and Berman's. We were girls then—no one
called us women—sixteen and yearning for everything,
sure that if we had money to buy all the glitter
and shine on those racks and shelves,
we would be happy.

We used to call it downtown, remember? It was fun
to go there, an outing with our friends where we
could chatter about school, boys, and after a few hours,
climb back on the bus for home. The world for us was simple:
those who had things and those who didn't—
all the things we were desperate to have.

Walking down Main Street, our bodies supple
and energetic, what did we know about what mattered?
What did we expect: that money clinking
into the cash register of the world would fill the closets
inside us that always were empty no matter how many things
we threw in? How could we know
then of the stream of losses, my husband
with his broken body, my daughter

15

with her broken heart,
my mother, father, sister all dead,
all the aunts and uncles of my childhood gone,
and I, who hate malls, never go shopping
if I can help it, think back
to a time when walking down Meyer Brothers' aisles
was all I needed to make me smile.

Why I Loved the Library

My mother, who never wanted me to leave
the front stoop, let me go to the Riverside Branch
of the Paterson Public Library. Each week, I'd climb
the steep hill, past the houses larger
and much nicer than ours—huge two-family houses
with big sun porches—I'd open the door into the library
and it was like stepping into another land,
one full of quiet, the soft muted colors
of the book covers, the well-worn pages, the hours
in the children's section, the chairs the perfect
size for me. Christine, the librarian, always welcomed
me as though I were an old friend. We spoke Italian
in the house and we had a set of encyclopedias
that my mother bought on time from a door-to-door
salesman, a set that my brother read all the way through,
but when I was eight, my sister got a book
of Grimm's Fairy Tales for a birthday present,
and she, like my brother, was very practical and scientific
and uninterested in fairytales. I loved that book
and once I had read it, I wanted more,
so I talked my mother into allowing me to go to the library
and enter that magical kingdom where I could spend
an hour surrounded by books, choose my books
by starting at A, working my way around the shelves.
When I was 11, Christine said, "Okay, you can move
into the adult section now." I can still see
the sunlight pouring through the large windows,
the exquisite stillness of the room,
the power that books possessed
to make me feel warm and safe in the same way
a bowl of pasta and chicken soup make me feel comfortable,
even today, all these years beyond childhood,
and the way I rushed home down the hill, clutching
my seven books for the week, all that treasure
I carried in my arms. I swear I was so happy
my feet didn't touch the ground.

17

Bookbags and Galoshes

My bookbag when I was growing up was made of canvas,
brown and ugly. I hated carrying it, and I remember
how it slapped against my leg as I walked to PS 18.

On rainy days, my mother made me put on black
rubber galoshes. I was a pathetic picture with my hair cut
by the lady who had a beauty shop in her living room.

She thought my hair was too thick and curly. She tried
to tame it by thinning it out with special scissors
and she cut it as though she were using a hacksaw.

I tried to erase the image of myself, the way even my skin
didn't seem to fit me, the way my eyes always looked
at the ground as I walked, the way even now,
22 years after my mother died, I can see her
and hear her voice as though I carry a DVD of her

playing in my brain, the way she'd button my coat
before I walked out the door, the hand-me-down coat
that belonged to my sister and was purple and red,
so I stuck out like a tacky flag even on a bleak, rainy day.

"Be careful," she'd say, and "hurry up, you don't want to be late,"
and then she'd fold me into her arms, kiss my cheek
and say, *come sei bella.*

And all the way out of the house
and down the walk toward the school,
I almost believed her.

In the Grammar School Graduation Photo, PS 18, Class of 1953 Graduates

The photographer posed us on the small lawn
in front of PS 18. We all wore dresses we sewed
in home economics, the ones that we worked on
in class all year and that Miss Burdy,
the Home Ec teacher, did not allow us
to take home until the week before graduation.
My mother was horrified.
The dress was all scratchy white lace,
but by the time I handed it to her,
it was dirty gray.

"What did you do?" she kept shouting in Italian,
though she washed it three times
before she could get it clean, and took out all the stitches
and sewed the dress again, so I wouldn't have to be
ashamed on graduation day.

There we all are, the 1953 graduates, the girls
in their white dresses with cap sleeves,
our dress-up shoes, mine with low heels.
All the girls have corsages pinned to their dresses.
Strange, how so many of these faces
come back to me now,
as though I had seen them all yesterday.

There in the back row is my best friend,
who already looks like a woman,
and Judy, beautiful as always,
who will marry a man who beats her,
have five children, gain 200 pounds and divorce
her husband only after he beats her so badly
she has to be in the hospital for three weeks.
There is sexy Miss Richmond, though I didn't
understand that's what she was then.
There's Herman Westfall, whose family

moved him out of Paterson, away from all
the Italian immigrants and their children
who surround him in this picture.
There's Joey Menturo, who was handsome
in a sleazy mobster way,
and beautiful John Wright, looking out of place,
John, whom I loved fiercely,
so handsome and blond and elegant.

In the moment when this photo is taken,
we are caught before we were anything more
than boys and girls. We lose track of one another,
though sometimes I meet one of them,
see in their faces so much of what they hide this day,
before high school, before college, before jobs,
before marriage and children, before success and failure.
We are full of hope, looking into the camera,
though we cannot see around the corner of time
to know what waits for us
in the years ahead.

The First Day of High School

On the first day of high school, I dressed carefully.
I picked out a plaid pleated wool skirt
and a white broadcloth blouse
and bobby socks and saddle shoes.

I wanted to look like a future college girl,
like an American middle-class girl. So when I
took the bus on Madison Ave. to Eastside H.S.,
and entered the wide double doors of the school,
I hoped I would be made new, could be friends
with the preppy girls, could leave behind
the cold-water flat, my Italian parents,
my world of no money.

Once inside the stone halls of the school,
I learned what I should have known—
that what I was, where I came from,
was marked on my face. All the preppy
clothes in the world couldn't disguise
my lower-class accent—the one a famous poet
told me I should get rid of, should hire
a voice coach to erase.

"No, I don't want to," I shouted, and I see myself
at 13 in my pleated skirt and bobby socks,
my Italian face contradicting my clothes,
and all the attempts I made to change myself,
to deny my family and all they gave me,
because it wasn't American enough for me,

and my rage at her is bitter as bile in my throat.
"No," I said again. "No, I don't want to,"
and I know nothing I say can explain
why I want to wave my past in front of this woman
like a protest banner.

In the Blue Stamp Redemption Center

My best friend, Janet, moved into town in 7th grade,
and became my friend by default.
Her mother died when she was 11, and her father
remarried. Her stepmother gave her a book
on becoming a woman and we both read it.

In 1952, sex was a mystery, a word to be whispered.
Yet, in the 8th grade Janet had a boyfriend
and told me jokes about sex and Vaseline.
I laughed though I didn't understand.

When we graduated, Janet and her family moved
to Pompton Lakes. One time I took the bus to visit her.
We sat near the brook in her backyard, ate watermelon
and walked through town. Janet told me
she had a new boyfriend and was in love.

The next year she came to visit me in Paterson
and we went to the Blue Stamp Redemption Center
to buy an iron. Her boyfriend was in the army.
They were going to get married, though sometimes
he didn't write for weeks and she worried.

I wanted to go to college, and after seeing Janet
I knew one thing—I didn't want a life like hers
of cookbooks and blue stamps, a life with this boy,
who sometimes didn't write to her,
a boy she needed because she thought
she had nowhere else to go.

The Clothes I Wore in High School

I have always had a disastrous sense
of style, and even when I followed *Seventeen*
magazine like a religion, I didn't know
what would work on my slender,
awkward body.

Unfortunately, I had thick, curly dark hair
that stuck out from my head, so it looked like
the beautician had deliberately formed it
into a triangle that swallowed my face.
I looked like what I was—a girl who did not speak
English when she first went to school—and all
the preppy clothes in the world could not change me
into an upper-middle-class girl,
who lived in a big white colonial house,

and not in a tenement on 19th Street that faced
the brick windowless wall of Warner Piece Dye Works.
The girls in *Seventeen* magazine would never have lived
in a house like ours—with its small kitchen,
its broken down bathroom, its tiny bedrooms,
barely large enough for a three-quarter bed,
and the living room with a sofa and two chairs

meant for company, but really all our company,
my honorary aunts and uncles and cousins,
came to the back door. We all gathered
at the dining room table—the adults playing cards
and talking and drinking espresso
and the children sitting on the sofa bed
or playing games on the linoleum floor.
In high school, I was in alpha classes
filled with upper-middle-class girls
with their expensive felt poodle skirts
and cashmere sweaters in pastel colors
and leather penny loafers. In those classes,

I learned to love the sound of poetry read aloud,
but I also learned that an enormous distance
separated me from the other alphas
who came in on Monday mornings talking about parties
they'd gone to or given in the finished basements
of their big houses in the Eastside section,
where the factory owners and professionals all lived.
I must have seemed so strange to them in my clothes
that were all wrong and my cheap haircut and my big nose.

I never spoke to anyone in the class
but when Miss Durbin called on me
to read a poem aloud,
I so loved the words,
sweet as a peach in my mouth,
that the girls and their parties vanished,
and I was left holding poems in my hand,
feeling the words rise off the pages,
lifting off toward the ceiling
like birds with glittering wings.

At the Factory Where My Mother Worked

Once when I was seventeen, I visited the factory
where my mother worked. It was on the second floor
up a flight of narrow, rickety stairs, and when I opened
the door, the noise of sewing machines slapped my face.

I searched for my mother in the close-packed row
of women bent over their sewing. The floor manager
picked up one of the pieces my mother had finished,
screamed, "You call this sewing?" and threw the coat

on the floor. The tables were lit by bare light bulbs,
dangling on cords. I had never seen the place
where my mother worked. She thought we should be
protected from all that was ugly and mean

in the grown-up world. "Children should be children,"
she'd say. "They'll learn trouble soon enough.
We don't need to tell them about it." She did not answer
the floor walker. Instead, she bent her head over her sewing,
but not before I saw the shame in her face.

Our First TV

We got our first TV when I was eleven. I was fascinated
by *Father Knows Best,* his big white house,
his huge living room and dining room,
the elegant stairs, his wife in her heels and dresses
and frilly white apron,
nothing like the homemade aprons
my mother wore, the ones she sewed from flour sacks
with their rough cloth and tiny flowers.

Before TV, I had the Dick and Jane books to teach me
about that other America with its big houses
and lawns, its pipe-smoking father raking leaves
in his cardigan and brown dress pants.
I loved those characters, the world they painted
so different from my own,
but it wasn't until the TV program
that I understood that my America—with its cold-water flat,
its small rooms, the life of making do, its Italian chatter—
was so different from upper-middle-class American life
and that my America was there in my accent,
in the expressions I used, in all I didn't know about life
in those white colonials in towns like Summit or Ridgewood.
In the half hour of the show, I could pretend
their world was mine, but some practical part of me knew
the distance was too great, and in the comfort
of my mother's house,
in the food I loved,
in the music of Italian,
I was where I belonged.

Years later, I dated a young man whose parents lived
in Scarsdale, and when he took me to their house
for dinner, they were horrified by me.
By then I had graduated from grad school
and was teaching at a college,
yet they knew I was not one of them.

Their maid poured my coffee and handed me
a silver bowl with tongs to pick up
the sugar cubes and I kept dropping them.
They all stared while I struggled.

His parents thought I was after his money,
and later, I learned they hired a private investigator
to look into my family. Even so, I was invited
to a cocktail party at his house, and his sister,
who graduated from Smith, had invited all her friends.
They all wore black cocktail dresses and black heels;
I wore a grey suit.
His sister came up to me in the middle of the party
and hissed, "You don't belong here. Can't you see that?
Leave my brother alone."
For the rest of the evening I barely held on,
my lips trembling, a fake smile on my face.
I told him I could not see him anymore.
I was too humiliated to say why.

All the TV programs in the world
could not have prepared me
for the invisible walls
that protected those people
from people like me.

The First Time I Saw My Mother Cry

Yesterday, I saw a snapshot of myself
taken in front of my cousin's house on 25th Street.
My cousin was 16 and dressed in an elaborate party dress;
my sister was 12, slender and beautiful
and already developed into a size 34D bra.
I sat next to my cousin in my imitation wool skirt
and cotton blouse, bobby socks and saddle shoes.
My eyes looked away from the camera.
My cousin Philip stood behind his sister,
dressed in a suit and tie. He was 13.

Of course, we could not know that Philip would shoot up to 6 feet
the next year, would be on the football team, would take
my little brother out for ice cream on Easter,
nor could we know that four days later, Philip
would get sick and die. That's the first time
I saw my mother cry, for who would think
that tall, broad shouldered, handsome Philip
would slip into a coma and close his eyes for good?

But for the moment, I did not know about any of that,
did not know enough to be grateful
for all I'd been given
and all that would be taken away.

Miss Cherry

At sixteen, I worked in the Paterson Public Library
on Broadway in Paterson, NJ—that building with its tall
columns and wide stairs, that building
with its marble halls and its bronze statues,
its large reading room,
its mahogany front desk
where Miss Cherry, the Head Librarian, presided,

Miss Cherry who hated me because I was a child of immigrants
and working class, Miss Cherry who looked down her nose
at me in my cheap nylon blouses and saddle shoes.
I hated her back, but I loved that library,
row after row of books, I loved the smell of them,
loved to touch the covers and the pages.

My job was to collect the returned books
 and cart them up translucent glass stairs to the stacks
and reshelve them. I was fast so I always had
a few minutes to read in the poetry section
and then I'd rush downstairs to collect
another armload of books to cart upstairs.
Althea, a tall, slender, beautiful black girl,
was also a library aide. Miss Cherry hated her

because she was black, but Althea was the daughter
of the owner of the largest funeral home in Paterson.
Miss Cherry, I realized years later, was afraid of her,
afraid of her family's success,
afraid to pick on the daughter of people
who had enough power to fight back,

but she knew that I had no one to protect me.
I was an easy target for Miss Cherry's mean tongue.
Althea said, "Don't let her talk to you like that,"
but I just ducked my shy head and showed up
every day for work and never answered back.
Then one day, I came in and told Miss Cherry

that I won the "Voice of America Essay Contest"
and I needed to go to City Hall to get my prize
and recite my essay. She was shocked silent.
When she recovered, she said, "I'll help
you practice," but she was the last person
in the universe I wanted to help me with anything.
For a while, at least, she wasn't mean to me,
although gradually she forgot
and went back to hating me,
as though I were dirt under her feet.

What I Always Wanted

As a girl, I wanted one of those large white
Victorian houses with the wrap-around porches.
I imagined the house as though it were actually mine.
The trim painted lavender,
the porch with its expensive wicker furniture,
wide-backed armchairs and rocking chairs.
I imagined plants hanging from hooks
along the porch roof, and a turret room
from which I could see the New York skyline.
I imagined life inside that house
with its curving stairs, its chestnut newel post,
its spacious rooms.

What I had instead was a tenement
on 17th street in Paterson,
four rooms with a small front stoop
and a back porch with stairs that led
to the 2nd floor apartment.
I remember the kitchen as a large room,
but looking back I realize it was only large
in comparison to the other three rooms.
In the center of the kitchen,
a wooden table covered by oilcloth
and wooden chairs placed near the coal stove
that heated the room
and on which my mother cooked our meals.
Our house was full of noise and laughter,
soup and gravy bubbling on the stove,
bread baking in the oven, at our table
there was always room for one more.

In that Victorian house, I imagined silence,
no honorary aunts and uncles sharing a meal
or espresso or anisette. What I wanted
was a life where my ancestors' photos

rested on a mantel in silver frames,
a champagne life, satin and taffeta dresses,
men in cardigans smoking pipes.

How I struggled to leave behind all the people
who made me who I am,
those people who taught me how to laugh,
how to reach out to others and welcome them.

Now that so many of those I loved are dead,
I realize how wealthy I was
in all the ways that mattered,
how a house, even a beautiful one,
cannot sustain me
like the memories of that love-lit kitchen,
the warmth of the people who called me theirs,
wrapped in a shawl soft as cashmere,
an exquisite and glorious one
that even today can soothe me
when I am most afraid.

II. All We Didn't Know

The Burgundy Pants Suit

I had a wool burgundy pants suit
with a tight fitting jacket and shell
and bell bottom pants that I liked to wear
to my job teaching in a high school.

One day in the English Department office,
I climbed on a chair to reach the top of a cabinet
and Ken, one of the English teachers, grabbed
me around the waist and buried his face in my back
and professed his love for me.

I was shocked by his tight grip and his declaration,
but I managed to pry his arms off me and shout,
"No, I'm married, you can't do this, I'm married"—
and if I wasn't so flummoxed I would have said, *you are, too.*
"Someone could come in. Get off me." Sure enough
the head of the department walked in
and we leapt apart.

I climbed off the chair, pretending nothing had happened,
scuttled out of the office in my burgundy pants suit
that I thought was so elegant, and that the cleaning lady,
I'd hired a few weeks later when I thought I'd collapse,
shrank it in the dryer, so it looked
like a pants suit to fit a doll.

Trading in the VW Bus

When we moved back to New Jersey,
we bought a house without seeing it on Oak Place
in Hawthorne across from my sister's house.
We drove to New Jersey in our VW bus,
and soon after we settled in,
my sister said, "Listen, you have to get rid of that bus.
The neighbors are talking. They think you're hippies,
and this is not that kind of neighborhood."
So we gave in, sold the VW camper and instead
bought a Ford Pinto station wagon,
dark green and sedate, unimaginative as mud.
I loved the VW bus, the camping trips we took in it
to Colorado, New Mexico and Arizona,
the table that turned into a bed,
the built-in booths that held sheets and blankets
and pillows, the board we placed across the front seats,
so John, who was only 4, could sleep on it,
and the crib we placed in the back for Jennifer.
Letting that VW bus go was an admission
we were no longer as young as we had been,
that we'd have to move into adulthood in a way
we had not before, a life of suburban homeowners,
just like that boring green Pinto, that car
that almost shouted *we are careful, frugal adults.*
Though we had just turned 30, we would have
liked to pretend we were flower children forever.

Bell Bottoms and Platform Shoes

A friend sends me a picture of herself
from the 70s—bell bottoms, platform shoes
a patterned button down shirt,
hair puffed up from a perm.

I can see the outline of the person she is now
and she reminds me of myself in the 70s—
married for eight years to a man
I knew I loved the moment I saw him,
two children who seem to me exquisitely
beautiful because they look like my husband
and not me.

The picture reminded me of all those evenings
when I dressed in bell bottoms and silky patterned shirts
and shoes with chunky heels. Those evenings
we'd invite friends over for drinks and conversation,
our children asleep upstairs. Those clothes, the perm
I got, because I wanted to be cool, though my hair
was already kinky, so the perm made me look
like I'd stuck my finger in a light socket.

I look at a picture of us from that time—Dennis and I
standing together at the head of the dining room table,
friends seated around us. Dennis's face is flushed,
his eyes shining. I wonder if he is tipsy.
He is wearing a fitted shirt with little flowers on it.
I am grinning and looking up at him. I might as well be
wearing a neon sign that says I love you.

Looking back at us, I would like to tell
my younger self—look how fortunate you are,
the man you love beside you, your children sleeping
in their safe beds, your friends around you.
Listen, be grateful for the moments
caught in these photographs,
the world full of possibility,
the sky not yet darkened.

Under the Grape Arbor

After dinner when I was a child we'd walk from 17th Street
up the hill to visit my aunt and uncle, Zia Rosa and Zio Gianni.
Zio built a huge grape arbor at least thirty feet long
and 20 feet wide down the center and lined up tables
covered in oilcloth. He built a bench
that ran all the way around the edges, where all
the children would sit. Zia Rosa would give us
cream sodas and cookies and the women would sit
at one end of the tables gossiping in whispers
and laughing. The men would sit on the other end
playing cards, talking politics, and drinking wine
in short glasses, peaches sliced into each glass.

My father and the other men all made their own wine,
and at the same time each year they made a trip
to the farmers' market to buy boxes of grapes. I remember
my father lugging those boxes into the basement.
He'd wash the grapes, feed them into the wine press,
and then transfer them to the wooden barrel
where they'd ferment, the aroma rising
through the floors into our cold-water flat.

If I close my eyes, I can still smell them.
My father poured the wine into green gallon jugs
to be set out on our dinner table, one bottle at a time.
Then, he would pour the wine into a short water glass
and he and my mother would have one glass with each meal.
We never got to drink this wine, except sometimes
at my uncle's house. My uncle made the best wine
of all the men, and he also made whiskey and liquor so strong
a tiny glass could send even larger men reeling,
and he'd encourage them to drink more than one
until they'd stagger home.

First Communion Photo

My friend tells me that her granddaughter
is having her First Communion. Her son married
a young woman from Spain and their child
is being raised in her religion, Roman Catholic.
When she tells her son that she won't fly down
to Florida for the Communion, he is upset.
She agrees to go, but since she was raised
Presbyterian she asks questions about the ceremony,
what gift she should buy, and asks me to bring in
a picture of my Communion. I can tell she is confused
by a ceremony that seems bizarre and exotic to her.

In the photograph, I am about 7 years old, and I am
standing in my backyard with Judy, my best friend.
Both of us dressed in frilly white Communion dresses,
veils on our heads like little brides. I do not mention
that my mother tried to sew a dress for me
from inexpensive, imitation satin, and when
my aunt saw it, she said, "No, you can't send her in that.
Go down to Jacobs and buy her a First Communion dress
or she will be humiliated," and my mother, who worked
in a factory earning 25 cents an hour for sewing
the linings in coats, bought the dress and veil for me
because, though she couldn't afford it,
she didn't want me to be embarrassed
in front of the other children, as she was ashamed
when my aunt pointed out that the cheap satin dress
she was sewing would have stood out as clearly
as if I arrived in a potato sack.
In the photo, Judy and I smile, our eyes squinting
in the sun. We are both slender, though Judy
is blonde and beautiful. I am dark-haired,
my face long, my eyes huge.

Years later, when we are both married, I meet Judy
at a church. She weighs 300 pounds,

has five children, and a husband who beats her.
Ten years later, Judy calls me. As she talks,
I remember the guy she dated in high school,
the one who was already beating her then.
I went to visit her when she had a car accident
that broke her arm and shoulder.

Only later, did I realize that this "accident"
was just like the doors she supposedly walked into
to explain her bruises and black eyes. On the phone,
she tells me she divorced her husband after the last time
he beat her. She was in the hospital for three weeks.

"I'm married again," she says, "My husband is
a good man, but I don't know,
sometimes I miss my ex-husband.
He was so exciting."

My Mother Was a Brilliant Cook

The first time my mother went out
to eat was on her 25th wedding anniversary
at Scordato's in Paterson, and the second time
was for her 50th anniversary
at the Iron Kettle House in Wyckoff.

My mother said, "I could have cooked
this meal better myself."
But I knew she was happy,
though she would have never admitted it.

Once my mother came to Paterson
from Italy in steerage,
she was content to stay there.
She was a brilliant cook,
and didn't need to go to restaurants.
She loved her house, poor as it was,
and never stayed in a motel or took a vacation
or wanted to.

She was content to offer platter after platter
of food to her family gathered
in her basement kitchen, and to watch them
laughing and talking together,
while she stood behind them
and smiled.

The Day I Lost My Daughter in Macy's

I had forgotten until now about the time I lost
my four-year-old daughter in Macy's shoe department.
I always hated shopping, but I was looking at a pair
of boots, trying to figure out whether they'd be comfortable
when I realized she was gone.

I ran through the racks of shoes, calling her name,
then circled wider, past racks of suits and sweaters.
Finally, I saw her and scooped her up,
untangling her from a glittery shawl.

All these years later, I wonder if she remembers being lost,
my voice sharp with fear, rising higher and higher
as I called her name. My practical, lovely,
down-to-earth daughter,
my daughter who always seems to know
the right thing to do,
who sees all too clearly her dippy mother
turning away from her, letting go of her hand.

I can almost see her rolling her eyes, her mother
too easily lost in a dream world or in a poem,
her mother who almost by accident,
raised this perfect daughter, this treasure,
this girl, who fills the room with light.

I Was a Good Italian Girl

I was a good Italian girl, quiet, shy, bookish.
I followed my mother's rules that lined up
like tin soldiers in my head; though I did refuse
to go to William Paterson to be a kindergarten
teacher as my mother wanted,
and instead went to Seton Hall to major in English
on a full, four-year scholarship.
I took 21 credits a semester, mostly in literature,
classes I loved that prepared me to be a poet,
though after the first time I mentioned
wanting to be a poet, the room filled with silence.
I never said it again. I knew I'd have to get a job,
have to support myself, have to pay
my own graduate school tuition.
All along, I read as many poetry books
as I could, but I could never get enough
of the language that roared inside me,
like the Great Falls in Paterson after days of rain.

I was a good Italian girl, followed
my mother's rules about what women
could and could not do.
I'd pick up the children from school,
cook dinner, wash clothes, iron and clean,
not that I was very good at being domestic,
but I always tried hard.
One day, I was supposed to wash the curtains
in my daughter's room, but when I came home from teaching,
I decided to apply for a NJ State Council on the Arts
fellowship in poetry. I started dinner,
but then, instead of taking my daughter's curtains down,
I typed up some poems, filled out the application,
made a thousand typos, and five minutes before
the post office closed, I mailed the envelope.

I never did wash those curtains that day, but six months later,
I got a letter telling me I had won the fellowship.
I've never been happier that I sent in those poems
and ignored my mother's voice in my head
saying that washing my daughter's curtains
was the most important thing of all.

How Many Hours

"The world is too much with us; late and soon,/Getting and spending we lay waste our powers:"—William Wordsworth

When the children were small, how many hours
did I push them in a shopping cart through the aisles
of Bradlees, because the walls of that tiny apartment
in married student housing were closing in on me,
because Dennis was in grad school and busy
and I had the children and I was lonely.

There was nothing I wanted in all those stacks
of objects—toasters and towels and blenders and sheets,
but I had to keep walking, counting off the minutes
and even in the grocery store where I had to go
even there I felt the minutes of my life draining away
while I waited in line and tried to keep
the children entertained.

Oh, all those endless hours, the grumpy looks
on the faces of the people in those aisles,
those people waiting as though
they were trying to fill the Grand Canyon inside them.
In these tacky aisles, there was nothing I wanted or needed
except this daily excursion that I used to prove
to myself that I could survive these mundane days.

How quickly our children grow and disappear
into their new lives. How much
we long to have them back
smelling of baby powder and shampoo.

Now, I try to avoid shopping
in big box stores, where the past slaps me
in the face, the memory of those forlorn moments
so long ago, when I walked the aisles
with my children in the cart and wished
for something or someone to save me.

Looking at Nature Through Glass

Looking out at the grounds
of the Loyola Retreat House,
I realize that I love nature best
when I see it through a window.
I remember reading once that Emerson
also loved looking at nature through glass,
though his essays make it sound
like he was rambling through woods.
I've always been a physical coward,
and now that I am a physical wreck,
I love watching through a window
the way nature dresses and undresses
according to the seasons.

When the children were young, you and I
used to take them camping with us.
I remember sitting around the campfire,
the children already asleep in the tent
and you off to the restrooms to shower.
I'd sit facing the fire, my back to the woods
and I'd jump a mile into the air every time
a twig snapped, figuring that a bear was going
to lumber out of the woods to attack me.
I was tense until you returned,
sure that if we sat together, I did not need
to be afraid, though why I thought that you
could wrestle a bear, I don't know.
I only knew with you there I felt safe.

One time we took a camping trip to Canada,
and in the night it started to rain, lightning
and thunder, the flashes illuminating the tent roof.
The tree that loomed over the tent
looked like a dangerous creature,
and I forced you to get out of your sleeping bag
and carry the children to the ladies room,

which was made of cement blocks,
and where I wasn't afraid
that a tree would crush us.
When the storm passed,
we carried the children back to the tent,
horrified by the felled trees that littered the path.
The next morning we were driving towards Toronto,
and I told you I was never sleeping in a tent again.
You, the Eagle Scout, didn't understand.

I love the drive up Rte. 17 west to Binghamton,
where from my car window, I can watch
the mountain forest flaunting its changing colors.
In my car, I don't have to worry
about lightning or deer ticks or rattlesnakes.
Protected from all the things that terrify me,
I can sit in the safety of glass and metal,
while my body sings
its own exuberant song.

What Blooms in Winter

My father-in-law, that sarcastic dragon, that mean-spirited
impatient beast, showed me his plant, a Christmas cactus
he loved, which grew large and bloomed and bloomed.
My father-in-law who criticized everyone except my son,
his first grandson, that boy who loved him enough
that he spent a few nights each week at his house,
just because he wanted to, my son who cried
at his grandfather's funeral, though no one else did,
not even his wife of 50 years. My father-in-law
who needed heart surgery, went
to Columbia Presbyterian and the day before
his procedure he did the New York Times crossword
puzzle and that night a resident took him off
his heart pills by mistake and he died.
When I look at my Christmas cactus, I think
of my father-in-law—and nurture it as if it were a child.

One morning, two years after your death,
I walk into the dining room and find
the Christmas cactus in full bloom.
The gray fog through which I have been moving lifts,
and my spirit glows bright as those red and pink flowers.
This is what blooms in winter, these memories,
treasured and stored, ready to greet us
when we least expect such grace.

In a Bookstore in Hobart, New York

Ma, though you've been dead for 24 years, you come alive
again in this bookstore in Hobart, NY. I can feel that you
are with me today, I see you in your cheap housedress,
stiff with starch, you in your homemade apron
made from flour sacks, you in your basement kitchen
with the cracked brown and yellow tiles, the Formica table,
the padded metal chairs, the 1950 Kelvinator,
the white enamel stove on which you cooked thousands
of meals for all of us, your children and grandchildren,
all of us returning to you for food and comfort.

You appear solid as you were in 1970, when my children
were young, and I see you in your need to work hard,
your busy hands, your quick and practical mind,
all those women who came before you, those women,
my grandmother and great grandmother whom I never met
except through you, Ma, through the way you taught me
how to love, how to keep moving even when I was
so exhausted I did not think I could go one step more.

I hear you saying, "Oh, come on! Stop feeling sorry
for yourself. You think you have it hard?
Just keep going," and I do, Ma, and how can I do
less than you did—you who worked in Ferraro Coat Factory
for years, you and the other immigrant women
sewing linings in coats for pennies apiece,
you who got up at four each morning to cook
and bake bread so dinner would be ready
when you came home from the factory, you who walked
the 12 blocks to the factory and back, even after you fell
on one of our skates and broke 14 bones in your foot.

You did what you had to do. Only after you had finished
your shift and walked home on that broken foot
did you go to the doctor who put a cast on it,
who said you could not walk on it for six weeks.

49

This was one of the few times I ever saw you cry,
and years later, you said, "What good does it do?
Tears don't change anything."

Brave warrior woman, energy coming off you
in waves, woman who never gave up,
woman who comes to me today
in this upstate New York town where you've never been,
as though I could actually call you back from the dead
to give me comfort
when I am most in need.

We Thought We Were Part of This Revolution

Today, I remember all the folk songs you sang to me,
the ones you played on records—Peter, Paul and Mary,
Bob Dylan, Pete Seeger, the protest songs, the love songs,
the plaintive melodies that so typified what we felt in the 1960s.

We went to Columbia to hear Pete Seeger.
How extraordinary it was to feel we were part
of the revolution he preached,
how sure we could change the world.

Listening to that music, we did what so many others
had done before us—marches and sit-ins and protest banners—
and in the middle of it, we fell in love, and our lives changed
but not in the way we thought before we said our vows
and had children and our worlds grew both wider
and smaller, these creatures we brought into the world,
needed our attention and we would have sacrificed
anything for them, all the marches and concerts,
and movies we loved. We'd give up anything
to make sure they were safe.

Now, the world we thought we could change has moved on,
and we mourn the way we've polluted the earth,
the way hatred divides this country, the way people
shout over each other across a chasm.

When Pope Francis appears before Congress,
he advocates our responsibility to the poor, the homeless,
our need to be good stewards of the earth, the air, the water,
and people respond from both sides of the political spectrum,
but the next day, nothing has changed.

The country I thought was the greatest country in the world,
as my father always said, may crack down
the middle and dissolve into dust.
But how can that be? How can we allow that

to happen, hating immigrants though
we are a nation of immigrants,
hating anyone who does not agree with us,
anyone who does not look like us.

The Vietnam War divided the young from the old,
split the country in two.
We thought we had healed those wounds,
and now, what songs can we sing
to save us, to save the world?

I Tell People I've Let You Go

At 3 a.m., I wake up in my hotel bed.
I reach out expecting to find you there,
though you died three years ago.
I tell people I've let you go,
but that is a lie.

Last night at the dinner party, laughing and talking,
I remembered those evenings when we hosted
such parties—all the laughter and food and conversation.
The sicker you became the fewer the parties,
until we moved the table out of the dining room
and moved in your bed and hospital equipment,
Hoyer lift and wheelchair,
the buffet strewn with pill bottles.

Here in this candlelit dining room,
surrounded by such warmth,
I am overcome by grief.
How long will it take
before the memory of you will fade,
the life I thought we'd have already vanished
and in its place, this silence, sharp edged
as a razor slicing through all my defenses.
No lie I can tell myself
that will make you alive again
and bring back the young couple we were,
all our lives before us, our faces lit from within,
all the things we didn't know waiting to drop
on our oblivious heads like nets.

Nepal

In Nepal the earthquake kills
thousands of people, though two survive
for days under piles of rubble.

In Baltimore, the rioters loot and burn;
their anger molten lava
that destroys everything in its path.

Did the people in Nepal expect the collapse
of the buildings, the streets?
Did they expect that the earth
in its terrible fury would open
to swallow them?

So much of our lives are like that.
We cannot predict what will happen,
the moment before the world burns,
the building collapses,

and, we, in our ignorance, going about
our ordinary lives do not hear the rumbling
of what is about to happen to us
and the world we knew.

Because

Because 152 people are killed
by suicide bombers and more than
200 people are injured in other blasts
in a period of two hours in the City of Light,
where the Arc de Triomphe glitters
in the background.

Because we are small and helpless
before such rage
and can no longer feel safe,
even in beautiful Paris with its cafes
and boulevards and public gardens.

Because there is no place to hide from those
who are so careless about life
that they don't care if they die
in order to destroy us.

The Signer at Nelson Mandela's Funeral

"The signer at Nelson Mandela's funeral is a fraud,"
says the headline. He is just moving his hands around
and not saying anything. He stands next to President Obama.

The signer explains, "I was having a schizophrenic
episode. I thought angels were shouting at me.
It was very distracting; my head was full
of so much noise I couldn't hear the speeches."

The organizers of the funeral fall over each other trying
to explain how they came to hire him. He was only $75 a day.
Signing usually costs $100 an hour and signers work
in pairs so one can be resting, while the other works.

No one can explain where they found this agency
that offered the signer for an event that thousands
attended and millions more watched on TV
around the world. Didn't anyone vet the signer or the agency?
What if he had taken out a gun and shot all the world leaders
who were on that stage?

"The angels were so loud," the signer said. "Their voices
were so high-pitched I didn't know what they were saying,
and I kept moving my hands hoping they'd stop so I could under-
stand enough to translate into signs all the words
I was able to hear."

Each Day I Try

Not to say yes to so many requests,
and just when I believe I've learned,
I hear myself saying yes again,
until my list of things to do becomes tall
as a mountain I have to force myself to climb.
There must be some compulsion inside me
that makes me say yes to one more reading,
one more workshop,
one more recommendation letter.

I wish I could learn how to spend lazy days
on a beach or at a spa. My mother
never sat still, never pampered herself.
That is what I learned from her, and this is what
I've taught my daughter by the way I behave.
Though I wish I hadn't.
I wish that I could have shown her
how to have another life,
lazy days in a hammock or porch swing,
and not one like mine,
my appointment book so crowded
it is difficult to read.

This Is How Memory Works

This is how memory works:
rain on an empty street, grace
that comes to us in moments,
a scrambled puzzle, we have to find
the pieces that fit,
the aroma of garlic and peppers
on a Sunday morning
in my mother's basement kitchen,
a field of sunflowers, tall grass
after a summer rain.

The Catskills in Mid-September

It's mid-September in the Catskills, not yet cold.
I know in a few weeks the trees will flame with autumn,
but today these trees have their own brilliance,
with their lush, dark green leaves.

In Binghamton, I look at the Susquehanna River,
and I am saddened to see the river so low.
Just a few years ago, a huge deluge caused the river
to flood this road and two shopping centers.
But now, it seems impossible that this
can be the same river
that roared over its banks.

As the weather swings from downpour
to drought, I know we are all to blame,
know there is so much that has to change.

III. A Season of Loss

My Sister Was the One

My sister was the one who did wild things,
the one who took chances,
the one who climbed trees and played baseball
with the boys on 25th Street after school.

My mother would search the neighborhood
for her every day. "Where is Lauretta?
Where is Lauretta?" she'd ask each child
on the street, and each would point
toward 25th Street and each time
my mother wanted a different answer
and never got one.

At my mother's funeral, someone told me
about my mother's search for my sister
and she said she'd ask my mother
where I was—my mother said,
"Ah, Maria, she's in her room reading a book."

I always got my adventures second hand,
my physical courage lacking, my athletic
ability non-existent. My sister took a trip
through Europe on her own when she was 19,
spent the summer in Italy when she was 20,
dated lots of boys, flirted and flashed
her incredible smile,
proud of her perfect teeth.

My sister saw a house as she was driving by,
stopped at the side of the road and called
the real estate agent. She bought the house
in less than half an hour.

My sister was practical and passionate
and fun loving. She always had a gaggle
of friends. I was quiet and introverted,
had two friends I kept for years.

My sister had adventures. I had the characters
in books for company. My sister loved bright
red and purple, loved to stand out.
I wore her hand-me-down clothes
whose colors seemed too flashy and bright;
I didn't want anyone to look at me.

Today, I decide I am tired of second-hand adventures;
I want to try all the things I've been afraid to do.
Oh, I have my own kind of bravery,
a bravery of the mind rather than the body,
but I want to be the person who takes chances,
the person who isn't afraid of heights
and water and small spaces.

But I know I can't change the person
I was born to be, and this resolution
to do one wild thing next week
won't last any more than the resolution
to lose weight or work less.
So I'll go home and read a mystery about a brave
lady detective, one who takes on the tough
guys, one who is capable of scaling a wall,
running miles in pouring rain
or chasing a murderer and catching him.

I'll take my adventures second-hand in my recliner,
the one I joke that I'm having an affair with,
because so often I fall asleep in its brown arms,
and dream about a fearless person,
the one I can admire
but can never be.

My Sister Loved to Dance

Ah, brutal irony, my sister who loved to dance,
climb trees and play baseball with the boys,
got sick with rheumatoid arthritis when she was 30,
all her love of movement and adventure
gradually taken from her, her feet twisted and deformed,
her fingers bent under, so her hand
looked like the body of a crab.

As a baby, she was beautiful, her skin white as camellias,
her cheeks rosy, her eyes large and chocolate colored.
As she grew up, she could not resist rushing up to 25th Street
after school to play baseball with my cousin and his friends.
Unafraid of rollercoasters and the Ferris wheel, she dragged me
behind her when she went with her friends
to Palisades Amusement Park, and I'd wait while they went
on all the rides I was too cowardly to go on.

At 19, she spent the summer in Italy, rode a donkey
down the mountain, climbed on the back
of Francesco's motorcycle, shocking the village
and causing a flurry of letters to my father,
letters accusing her of being wild.

After she married and had children, she still loved
adventure, danced all night on a ship
to the Land of the Midnight Sun,
went on trips all over Europe, Russia, China.
Even after the disease began to attack her body,
she took trips to exotic places, hired a driver
when she could no longer walk.

Each day she went to work as a nurse in my brother's office,
hired an aide to take her there in a wheelchair.
Only at the end was she afraid.
She'd call me to come to her house each night
and we'd sit in her small den, she in her hospital bed

and I next to her, and I'd hold her hand, so fragile,
a hand I worried I'd break if I held it too hard.

Finally, she had to give up, let go of my hand, let go
of her life, even breathing was too much for her,
but she remains in my mind as that fire, that presence,
that unsinkable explosion of strength and energy and plans,
that indomitable woman who would try anything.

How Sad I Am Today, How Lonely

On this glorious October day, the sky scrubbed clean,
the clouds skittering across it,
that crisp scent of autumn air, no hint yet
of the winter that roars towards us,
I drink in the fresh taste of the leaves that have
just started to catch fire with their fall colors.
But, sometimes, despite the beauty,
I wear my sadness like a tattered coat,
my loneliness like a translucent veil.

Though I shed them both when I think of my daughter
driving from Massachusetts towards me.
Know that I will get home first.
When she comes in, bringing light with her,
her voice, her laugh, her smile
will be the gift that will lift this sorrow,
her hand the one that will lead me
out of that sad country
where too often now I live.

They Say I Have My Mother's Eyes

In the photograph, I see my mother
sitting at the dining room table.
When I look closer, I realize I am the woman
at the table, my head tilted sideways,
caught in mid-laughter.

People tell me I look like my mother,
though I had not realized it until now,
when I mistake my own face and body for hers.
I have the same energy she had, my body
always twanging with a desire to move.
She was practical and though I am a poet,
I too am rooted, make "to do" lists,
but never write them down, tick them off
in my mind as I complete each task,
like she did.

My mother would call on the phone
when my children were young,
and ask after each of us,
then suddenly, she'd be gone—no goodbye,
just click and she wasn't there.
I asked her why she didn't say goodbye,
and she said, "I found out you were all fine.
That's all I needed to know."

Sometimes, it's years before we realize
that we do something
because our parents did it that way,
and I know that's why I need to check
on my daughter even when I don't
have anything to ask her,
and like my mother I need to know
only that she is okay.

When I hear her voice, I think of my mother calling
our phone and getting the answering machine
with Jennifer's message on it,
and my mother's voice: "Oh Jennifer, your voice
is so beautiful, oh so beautiful,"

and even though that message was left
by my mother more than twenty years ago,
I can still hear the love in her voice,
the way she would have reached out
and hugged Jennifer if she had actually been
in the room with her,
the way even when she criticized me,
when she was too busy to say goodbye,
I always knew her love was the shawl
she gathered around us, softer than silk,
that shawl she knew we'd carry with us always,
even after the funeral procession led us
to Calvary Cemetery and that mausoleum
she insisted we file her in, because she was afraid
we'd forget to take care of her grave
and people would criticize us.
So she, who loved the feel of the earth
on her hands, chose the sterile mausoleum,
because even from beyond the grave
she was determined to protect us
from the neighbors' sharp tongues.

What the Body Knows

I tell my students they have to be vulnerable
as peeled grapes if they want to write,
and this morning, sitting in the IHOP,
I am quivering and exposed
as a peeled grape myself,
my eyes filling with tears,
my daughter's voice on the phone
flat and toneless as a straight line,
though I feel how much effort it takes
for her to say anything at all.
When she hangs up, I know
it is because she is crying
and can't speak. Earlier, I held

my friend's daughter, her blonde hair
pressed to my chest, my hand on her sweet
head, her eyes huge and lovely as pansies
after rain, and I remember holding
my daughter at three in the same way,
this sweetness that rose off her,
and I think how my body keeps inside
itself the sensory memory of holding a child,

how clear that child is to me, though
she is grown now and alone
in her Cambridge apartment,
and how when I held her
and she fell asleep in my arms,
I was so young, I thought this damp
and delicate weight
was all I'd ever have to bear.

My Daughter Forgives Her Father

I lied to myself about those rocky years of our marriage,
the children still in grammar school. I convinced myself
that they didn't know, though our arguments
were loud enough to wake the dead. We were
like two sides of an electrical charge. Sometimes we'd
spark off each other with an anger so violent
it could have broken a bone; then we would fly back
towards each other as though our bodies were magnets
that could not stay apart. Maybe we needed
the arguments to make the explosion of love

between us, but I did not want to believe
that the children knew, though sometimes
you would become so angry that you'd bang
your fist on the wall or hit your own head with your fists.
You tried to escape your father's voice listing everything
that was wrong with you. I tried to fix what was broken
inside you, tried to meet your anger
with my own, but your rage terrified me and no matter
how much I tried not to, I'd end up crying.

I hoped the children didn't know, but years later,
when I visit my son and his wife, she tells me
that my son hates his father, and I try
to make excuses for you, say how this terrible
illness has changed you into a man
John would not recognize—tender, gentle, courageous,
one who faces his disease without complaint, one who
never gives up. But John cannot forgive you.

Our daughter visits us as your illness takes away
more and more of what you can do,
swim laps, run for an hour at a time, ride your bike.
Now, you are caught in your electric wheelchair
and when you see her, your face is bright.
She cannot stay angry at you. I know

she has forgiven you for those tumultuous rages,
know she sees all too clearly
how you have changed. I wish I could go back

and erase some memories from our son's mind,
wish I could make him understand
that we did the best we could, that even though
we made mistakes we loved them, wanted them
to be happy, that you did not intend to frighten him,
as you frightened me. Those days are so long ago,
that what I remember is you holding Jennifer's hand
and you reaching out to smooth my hair,
the furious you so long gone
that I have to work hard to bring you back
the way you were when we were young.

My Daughter at 2

At 2, my daughter was graceful as a dancer,
her head covered in gold curls. Once a friend
made her a bright blue dress with a matching purse,
and I took a picture of her in the backyard
in Overland Park, Kansas. I could not believe
how beautiful she was,
her face tilted toward the sun, her eyes so blue
they could be sapphires.

My daughter at 46 is in love. For so long,
she felt betrayed by love,
and would not venture out of the safety of her condo.
But when she met Stephen,
she seemed transformed.

She sends a picture of herself with Stephen and his children.
Indigo, his little girl, is holding onto her arm, and Atticus,
his son, at 12, looks almost grown up, his shoulders
growing wide, his face, a younger version of his father's.
Indigo could be Jennifer's daughter, even though
she isn't, and I think back to Jennifer at 2,
when I see Indigo posing, her hand on her hip,
a feather boa wrapped around her shoulders,
and I think of Jennifer,

how she looked when I took that picture
in the Kansas sun and of Jennifer, 11 years married,
Jennifer walking into my arms and sobbing, all the golden
glow that lit her up at 2 and at 16 and on her wedding day,
all of it gone, and now, once again, her face so luminous
when she looks at Stephen, her hand in Indigo's hand,
her arm on Atticus's shoulder.

It's My Gillan Pot Roast

My daughter is working on her book, which was due
at the publisher weeks ago. She has not slept in days.
She tells me: "I am a Gillan. Remember grandma,
and how she'd start getting ready to cook a pot roast at 8 am
and by 5 pm she still wouldn't be finished? That's what I'm like
with this book. It's my Gillan pot roast." We both laugh,
but I hear the desperation in her voice.

I dig out my mother's rosary, begging God to send her
the energy and inspiration to find her way
to the end of this book. I haven't been to church
in years. I don't know why God would listen to my prayers
but for my daughter I am willing to try anything.

I promise all sorts of things if only God will help her
get the book finished so she can move on
with her life. Every day I call her.
Every day she is not finished. I tell her I am praying.
I can tell she is encouraged, but when more days go by,
she tells me, "Forget it. I don't need a prayer. I need a miracle."

I want to say: *It's a scholarly book. Three people
will read it. Why are you worrying? Just forget it.*

Instead she says: "You would have
finished it months ago. You're a Mazziotti.
This is my pot roast. I have to cook it
the Gillan way."

What I Can't Tell My Son

That I wait for his call every Sunday night,
though I pretend to myself that I don't care.
I have lost the easy way I once had with him,
the nights I sat at the edge of his bed
and we'd talk in the soft dark of his bedroom
until he fell asleep, that time when I felt so close to him
we could have been in one skin.

But now his own children grown, it's as though
a stranger has come to inhabit his body.
I struggle to find a story that will make him laugh
or some anecdote that will interest him.
I can't tell my son that I cry often after these calls,
can't tell him how much I need to hear his voice,
can't tell him I can still feel his high cheekbones
under my hand, still remember his heavy head leaning
against me as I read to him when he was a child.

I wonder what words he holds back.
Is he sad, too, when he hangs up the phone?
Yet, even these 10-minute phone calls,
these painful, awkward attempts at touch,
even these I do not want to give up,
so that if he were five minutes late with his call, I'd worry
and when the call is over, such loss I feel, such loss,
this son I will never stop loving,
though I am afraid sometimes
that if he were to walk into a room
I would no longer recognize him,
and I do not have the courage to ask him
if these calls are as painful and necessary for him
as they are for me.

In the Photograph from Summer Camp

Our children are six and eight. The photograph
was taken at the camp, which I paid for by driving each day
from our working-class neighborhood to Upper Saddle River.

I wanted the children to have what I never had,
so I suffered through a summer of driving
one-hour, round-trip, twice a day with three
other children besides my own,
three children who were rich and obnoxious
and one so gross I wanted to throttle her
with her conversation about rubbers that luckily,
none of the other children understood.

In the photograph, they are caught in a moment
of perfect and incredible beauty.
What I didn't know then was how much
would happen to them in their lives,
how I would hold my daughter while she cries,
how far away my son would grow from me.

But here they are in this frame, untouched
by betrayal and loss,
and on that day, sun rays glinting off their hair,
we did not know how forty years later this picture
would make me smile each time I pass it,
the memory so fresh in my mind as though
by giving them those days at that summer camp
I could guarantee them a future
showered by stars.

Grief

I have been grieving for a long time now.
So many of those I loved gone.
I remain behind in a house
that's suddenly too big for me.
I hide out in the back room,
sit in my brown recliner,
the kind I've always hated
because it smacks of illness and old age.

Now, I joke I am having an affair with my chair
with its pillowy, velvet arms, the way
it welcomes me home, the way I fall asleep in it
as though I were a child and it were a cradle.

I have been grieving for a long time now,
wish I could call you all back
and, sometimes, I imagine you are with me,
in my dreams you seem so alive,
you come to comfort me,
though when I wake up, you have vanished.

But I am learning gratitude for another April,
the world in its radiance dancing into spring,
and I am here to greet it,
my arms open, my feet
doing their own quiet dance.

Even Now, I See You

Even now, I see you though you are
four years dead. You are the shadow
in the corner of the room. You are the figure
who stands at the side of our bed. I feel
that you want to tell me something, but I don't
know what it is. These visits remind me
of the visits our dead family members made
to you when you were dying, but I am not dying,
at least I don't think so—so much left
to do, I think though that the practical part
of me knows it's not up to me
to decide how long I'll live.

My friend tells me I have to live my life, and I think
I have. Most days my life unwinds
like a ball of yarn behind me,
and I do not think of you,
but at night, sometimes in the bed we shared
all those years, you come to me.
I'd like to tell you what is happening with me,
with the children and grandchildren,
though I assume you know without my having to tell you.

It is my own need that pulls you back to me for these visits,
though now the outline of your figure seems diffuse,
like a pencil drawing that is gradually being erased.
My aching shoulder reminds me how grateful
I must be for the life that rages in my blood,
for all the serene and peaceful moments
that almost make up for
all that is lost
and can never be reclaimed.

Christmas Eve at Our House

For years, we gathered at my house for Christmas Eve, the entire
family and their assorted spouses and children
and grandchildren, extra friends who had nowhere to go.
My daughter and I would cook and bake and set the tables,
the tables placed end to end so they extended through my big
dining room into the living room, and we'd light candles,
and my sister-in-law, Janet, would bring her deviled eggs
and pies she had baked, and my mother would bring meatballs
and sausages to go with the lasagna we made, she'd bring fish,
five varieties, and sfogliatelle and struffoli, covered in honey
and sprinkles, the house so full of laughter and talk,
all of us happy and together. Then my mother died,
and my father, and after my sister died, her husband
sold their house across the street from mine and moved to North
Carolina and his daughters did, too. My son had moved years
before, and I put the extra tables away, took the leaves out
of the dining room table, and now we have to remember
we no longer have two dozen people for dinner. Instead,
we have six, including myself. Christmas Eve is lovely,
but sad—my mother and her food long since eaten,
I exist on memory, and we who remain behind to tell stories
of former holidays, when the children were young, when you,
my darling, were still alive, when mom and dad were still here
to tell stories, my sister, who made every party a party with her
exuberance, her quick wit, her big smile, qualities that the rheumatoid
arthritis couldn't dampen until it finally killed her. This year,
the six of us will sit around the table and we will be happy
remembering the past and the people who made
this holiday what it once was, and the missing tables
and empty chairs will float in the room around us,
while we pretend nothing has changed.

Oak Place, Hawthorne, NJ

In 1972, we moved to Oak Place.
At one time, the neighborhood was a park,
so it looked like a country lane,
oak branches leaning over the street
to form a canopy of lush green leaves.

But Oak Place no longer has any oaks.
The hundred-year-old trees that lined the street
have long since been felled by storms or neighbors
annoyed by falling leaves and acorns.
My neighbor's yard with its Japanese cherry trees
and evergreens was leveled off, planted with grass.
Now, I look out my window at a hot tub, brown and ugly.
No more explosions of blossoms in spring,
no more lilacs, hyacinths or lilies of the valley.

Is it any wonder I am startled when two bucks
show up at midnight on my lawn nibbling grass
in the moonlight, their bodies muscular and lithe,
the way your body once was.

I know that you died five years ago, that your body
is ashes in a box, but I want to believe your spirit
is inside these incredible creatures
and you have sent them to comfort me
as I walk this silent house.

The Dead Sit Calmly Among Us

The dead sit calmly among us.
I imagine them, their bodies back
the way they were when they were young.
Their faces patient and content, they wait
for us to notice them. We have gone
on with our lives
while they exist in that other place
and may return occasionally to visit,
as they did to my husband when he was
getting ready to die.

All his dead and mine joined him there
in the dining room, emptied to fit his bed,
his chair, the Hoyer lift, the electric wheelchair
and all the other contraptions
of the nearly dead.

"They were all with me last night," he said,
"My mother and father and yours, and your sister.
They were happy to see me.
It was like those old Christmas Eve dinners,
everyone here, talking and laughing."

Now, I imagine I see them all too,
but I keep this to myself. And you,
you whom I've loved so many years
that I thought I could not live without you,
you are already gone five years, your ashes
waiting in a brown box surrounded by pictures
of you, of us, of our children.

You have stopped visiting me. At first, you came
to see me often to give me comfort,
and then gradually your image faded
and disappeared.

I want to believe you are still sitting calmly
among us, that I could reach out my hand
and touch the high cheekbone of your face.

When I go, I tell my daughter, buy another box
and put me in it, then scatter
my ashes along with dad's
in the nature reserve behind your house,
or plant us in your garden under a rosebush.

When you look at the blooms
you will know
I am thinking of you.

When I Look at the World

When I look at the world outside, it is a study in gray
and white, the snow, that only yesterday was pure
and untouched, looks grimy, people's footprints follow
their own zigzag path across bumps of soft snow. The sky
is bleak, pale gray, utterly lonesome. Spring seems very
far away. This landscape with the mountain in the distance
wears a coat of leafless trees. The bark looks like black
lines drawn by a child. The world outside
is a mirror image of my life since you've been gone,
a study in gray, shrouded in sameness, the house
so empty it almost echoes. When we
were young, we'd lie in bed, my head on your chest,
and I'd listen to your heart beating.
In the brown recliner, where I sometimes sleep now
when our bedroom is too full of memories of you,
I hear my own heartbeat, it pounds
in my ears or maybe I only imagine that I hear it
because the house without you feels like a place
where not even the living move.

In the Classroom at Wayne State, Detroit

The students are crowded into a space
too small for all of them,
but they are doing what I asked.
Their pens move across their notebooks.
I want them to write the best poem
they've ever written, one that is filled
with the truth they've been afraid to know,
one that will change their lives,
like the woman at the reception the other day,
who told me I had changed hers,
and now, when I look at the bent heads
and concentration of these students,
I hope some magic will happen
in this classroom today, some spark
that will turn ordinary words into stars.

Today the Forsythia

Today the forsythia along Rte. 287 in New Jersey bursts
into bloom, the trees soften, their winter branches begin
to bend, move now more gracefully, supple and bouncing
in the early April breeze. The weather forecaster predicts
rain and snow for tomorrow, but this Thursday afternoon
it is spring, this endless winter behind us.

Even the conservatives are almost willing to admit
that climate change is real and that maybe, just maybe,
people might be responsible. I love the bright yellow
of the forsythia, the tulips someone has planted
at the town library, the crocuses that poke out
of the earth, though I am afraid

that these signs, the earth reborn, are false prophets
that can't cover up the dioxin polluted Passaic River,
the noxious odor of decay that pours forth
out of the landfill, the lots in Paterson where they have
buried toxic waste, covering it with white gravel.
It looks like a moon landscape surrounded
by a high wire fence that reads, "Danger. Do not enter."
I try not to breathe when I drive past, though families
live right across the street. Maybe it doesn't matter
to the people who decided to bury the toxic waste here
in the middle of a neighborhood of poor people.

I want to believe in the bright promise
of the crocus, the forsythia's yellow arms,
the new softness of the air,
but grief curls itself around my throat,
burns my eyes.

Last Evening in Vestal, NY

Last evening, I hear the peepers' wild chorus
for the first time this spring. But this morning,
the world is shrouded in thick fog,
I remember, so many other mornings,
fog dense as smoke,
and that moment when it suddenly lifts,
and the sun blazes, painting the earth gold.

My friend has lost the man she loved
and she tells me she has to get through
each day, one at a time, because otherwise,
it would be too difficult to go on,

and I say, "Listen, what will happen is
one day you'll forget to think
that a day has passed;
instead two days will pass without thinking
despair, despair,
and then three days,
until finally, like the sun after fog,

you will let go of this grief
and you will celebrate, once again,
the small fingers of the crocus poking out
of dead earth, the forsythia's
yellow arms waving,
the baby who smiles at you
though he has never seen you before,

all the small blessings that we can see again,
sharp and clean and joyous
as the peepers' insistent song.

IV. Lemons and Roses

I Come From

I come from the Riverside section of Paterson, NJ,
with its two- and three-family houses built close together,
separated by raggedy alleys that led to the back doors
where everyone, even company, entered.

I come from old ladies sitting on stoops in their black
mourning dresses, ladies who used big white handkerchiefs
to wipe the sweat from their brows
and to fan themselves in the humid August air.

I come from raised voices and laughter drifting
out of tenement windows,
the houses leaning into each other,
the old windows loose and rattling.

I come from a place where we knew everything
about our neighbors, but no one ever said anything,
at least not to their faces, but word spread
about the family arguments, the man who drank,
the married woman who invited a man
into her house in the afternoon.

I come from a place where we sat
around the kitchen table and talked and ate
and played Monopoly or dominoes.
The kitchen was where we did everything,
surrounded always by the aroma of baking bread
or sugar cookies and boiling soup.

I come from a place with so much love—
even today, I am grateful,
though I didn't understand all that I had
till it was gone.

The Italian Pilgrim

In the old photograph, we are standing
in front of PS 18. I am next to Charlie Linfante.
We are dressed as pilgrims, he in a hat
made of cardboard, and I in a long skirt,
a frilly apron, a white blouse, a paper Pilgrim collar.
My hair reaches my shoulders, my face
long and narrow, my eyes enormous in my thin face.
Charlie, who is Italian, but doesn't look it with his
blond hair and blue eyes, could actually
have been a pilgrim, but I look ridiculous.
I look foreign. My head is bent.
I look up at the camera as though
I am drowning. Whose idea was it to turn
the class of immigrant children into pilgrims?

Oh, you poor inarticulate dolt, how you wanted
to be an American, though even you in your naïveté
could not have thought you could be a pilgrim.
Years later, you will fall in love instantly with the man
you would later marry, his blond hair, his large
gray eyes, the high cheekbones of his handsome face,
but I wonder now, looking back,
if that was part of the attraction, his educated parents,
his large white colonial house like the ones
in the Dick and Jane books. Did I think he would
turn me from that Italian girl I was into an American,
that no one would notice my Italian face,
my lower class accent, my long curly hair
that frizzed up in the rain?

How I wanted to erase everything about myself
that I hated. I had my nose done, believed
if I could just have a small nose
all the parts of me that didn't fit would vanish.

It would be years before I'd recognize all I'd lost
in trying to leave behind the Italian that was
in my blood, electric and necessary,
and a part of me
I could never change.

Ancestors

The people who live only in photographs
line my mantel, my husband Dennis's
great-grandmother and great-grandfather
in their Victorian clothes, the women
in wide-brimmed fancy hats and long gowns;
the men in black suits and formal ties.
The small silver frames that circle the photos,
the chiseled faces of Dennis's ancestors,
his grandmother with eyes like my daughter's,
his grandfather who has my son's high cheekbones.

My father and mother also have a place
on the mantel, but even in their photos
it is obvious they are not from the same social class
as my husband's family. This summer in Italy,
I see a picture of my mother's mother and father,
both small-boned and slender, both working
in rocky fields, their faces worn and old looking
in the light of that unforgiving Mediterranean sun.

I am ashamed that I am grateful that my children
look more like Dennis's side of the family,
though my daughter claims that the other students
at Georgetown knew she was not one of them,
that she had tacky hair and the wrong clothes,
and I argue, thinking of how incredibly exquisite
she was at 18, her golden coloring, her long, shimmery
hair, her eyes the color of violets, her long lashes,
her delicate voice, all the grace tracing
a straight line back to the upper class ancestors
in the sterling silver frames. When she looks
in the mirror, she sees my ancestors, thinks she is
lower class because I am, and nothing I say
convinces her that my class is not hers,

that the private schools and lessons and slumber
parties and suburban house mark her
as my own background marks me.

I wish I knew how to convince her to value
her own beauty, to realize how her face is lit
from within like one of those seashell lamps
they sell at the Jersey Shore.

My Father Leaves Galdo, Italy at 16

In the picture of my father, taken at a studio
when he was 16, he is standing next
to a mahogany table, on it a bouquet of flowers.
He is small and slender, he wears a dark suit,
a sedate tie. He is handsome
with his thick black hair and pale white skin,
his face serious. He does not smile.
The picture was taken the week before
he left Galdo for America. He wouldn't see
his mother again until 14 years later
when he went back to Italy to find a wife.

His mother was to have arranged with my mother
to pay a call on them, but his mother
was a little scatterbrained. She forgot to let them know,
and when they arrived at my mother's house,
my mother was trying to capture the pig
who had escaped from the yard. My father tells us
when we are at Sunday dinner, so many years later,
that he knew as soon as he saw my mother chasing
that pig that she was the one for him.
"Her cheeks were red," he said. "She was beautiful."

My mother would shout from the kitchen,
"Don't tell about the pig again. Why do you
have to tell about the pig?" But my father smiled
and winked, "Beautiful she was," he said.

My grandmother carried my father's picture
from that time when he was 16 in her pocket
until the day she died at 92, though she had not seen
my father for more than fifty years.

My father sent packages of coffee and chocolate
and sugar and clothes at least once a month,
and blue air mail letters.
He didn't have the money to go to Italy;
she didn't have the money to come to America.

After her funeral, they sent my father the worn,
creased photo that she carried with her,
as if the picture could bring
her only son back to her.

My Father Was a Young Man Then

Only 16, when he came from Italy alone,
moved into the Riverside neighborhood
full of Italians from Cilento—all of whom
spoke the same dialect, so it was as though
they had transported those mountain villages
to Paterson. At first, America was terrifying,
English, a language they could not master,
but my father was a young man
and he became friends with other young people
and they learned how to take buses and trains
or to borrow a car, and off they'd go
on the weekend to Rye Brook or Coney Island,
free from their factory jobs on the weekends,
reveling in the strength of their bodies,
the laughter and music and the company.

My father was a young man then,
and even when he died at 92,
he never lost the happiness
that bubbled up in him,
the irrepressible joy of being alive,
the love of being with friends.

I imagine him in that time
before he married my mother,
before we were born,
before he had a tumor on his spine
that left him with a limp.
Imagine him with his broad smile,
his booming laugh, his generous spirit,
his sharp intelligence,
imagine him as a young man,
his head full of dreams,
his love of politics and math,

the way he carried those qualities
all the way into old age,
though his legs failed him,
though his body grew trembling and frail,
his mind never did.

When I'd arrive at the house
all those years after mom died, he'd smile
at me with real pleasure,
the young man he was at 16 would emerge,
sit in the room with us
and laugh.

Laura, Today I Am in South Dakota

Laura, today I'm in South Dakota and the sky, dark
and enormous, threatens with clouds, huge and tinged
by the setting sun, deep pink in a fat strip of ribbon.
Laura, I wish I could call you back from the dead,
could share with you the rare beauty
of this place so different from New Jersey.

Remember the summer you took a cruise with your husband
to the Arctic Circle and how you danced all night
on the deck of the ship. How excited you were
when you described it. Laura, I think of you as a young
woman, your clear skin, your chocolate eyes,
your wide mouth, your perfect teeth, your smile
that lit up a room. How you loved to travel and did
until you became too ill to go anywhere,
and too ashamed of the way the rheumatoid arthritis
twisted your hands and feet. Oh, when you were a girl,
I remember your size 5 feet in high heels,
your slender legs, the way you twirled
across polished floors.

Laura, I wish I could have taken you with me
to Sicily, where I've been invited to read.
What fun we could have had.
How the Sicilians would have loved you.
How you could have translated
my broken Italian into perfect speech.

Remember when mom was dying and she saw
her mother and sisters in a garden lined with white paths
and filled with light. If I can't have you here with me now,
I hope you are there with mom and her mother
and sisters and dad, hope your hands
are once again straight and perfect,

your smile beautiful,
hope there is a big dance floor and music playing
and you are happy
and your body is once again graceful
as it was when you were young.

When I Think of This Summer

When I think of this summer in San Mauro
that southern Italian town in Cilento,
where you grew up,
I imagine I could still see
the amazing vistas,
the hill towns and their houses
that look like Monopoly houses strung
along a mountain, the sky vast
and the sea miles below
the curvy mountain roads.

I try to imagine you as a little girl
walking the cobblestone streets
and sitting on the balcony of your house
to watch the clouds skitter across the sky,
the storm that rolls
in over the sea. I imagine
you loving the openness of living
on top of the mountain, watching
the stars in that enormous sky,
imagine that once,
when you were very young perhaps,
you had time for dreaming.

But after third grade you had to leave
school and you became the cook
for your family of nine. You'd serve
everyone breakfast, pack a lunch for them,
and after they left the stone house
you'd get dinner ready
and climb the steep mountain to the fields
where you worked all day beside your family.
At night, you'd leave first, because the sky
was starting to darken, so you would be home
to finish preparing dinner.

"I was nine years old," you told me,
"and sometimes I was afraid walking down
the mountain by myself, and once an old man
tried to grab me but I ran away."

Today in this town that I have come to love,
I conjure my mother up, wish for her a life
of leisure and plenty she never had,
wish she could join us here at the San Mauro
bed and breakfast, called Magico Orizzonte,
and where we would breathe in the mountain air,
clear and clean as water, where my grandson says
what I've been thinking: "It makes me feel so free."

Time, a Waterfall of Minutes

It's almost November, yet if I close my eyes, I can see
San Mauro, that small Italian town on the top of a mountain
where my mother was born and where
this summer they hosted an event in my honor.

Professor Marracco came to pick me up at the bed and breakfast,
and drove me to the town square. There, the mayor
took one of my arms, and my grandson the other,
and we marched up the hill, while the town band played.
At the top of the hill, five old men removed their hats,
and stood up to honor us. The mayor led me to a chair
in the front row, where my grandson and translator sat,
and some first cousins, including the one who is now blind
and was the postmistress for years. She held my arm and cried.

Professor Marracco started the ceremony, and students
and professors read my poems in Italian. One by one,
people asked for a copy of the book with my poems
that described my mother and the town and people she loved.
Then, the mayor took my arm and led me to the house
where my mother was born, and on the front of the house hung
a red cloth. He told me to pull it and I did—and there
was a plaque with my name and my mother and father's name.
My mother was shy and would have been uncomfortable
with all the attention, but my gregarious father
would have been thrilled as he was when I read
at the United Nations, and he stayed up until midnight
watching TV, sure I'd be on channel 4, though of course, I wasn't.

After the ceremony, people lined up to speak to me, have me sign
their books. I could have almost floated away, I was so happy,
here in this beautiful place, where I imagine
my mother and father are with me,
breathing when I breathe,
smiling when I smile.

Be a Human Fly

I couldn't climb the ropes in gym,
"Try again," Mrs. Dey yelled,
and I did, but I'd always fall off,

and, sometimes, I imagine I am trapped
in a burning room and the only way
to escape is to climb a rope
to the roof but even the thought
of turning into a smoking ball of fire
can't make me climb the rope.

Once in gym class, Mrs. Dey said:
"I want you all to be human flies.
Put your back to the wall, your hands
on the floor, and then climb backwards
up the wall with your feet."

"I can't do it." I said. "I'm Italian. My mother
wouldn't like it. I might get hurt,"

and I wasn't lying. My mother
would have been afraid for me,
like the only time we went to the beach,
and every time I went near the water,
my mother screamed, "Watch out! You'll drown."
My husband tried to teach me to swim. I almost
drowned him. "Never again," he said.

I tell my friend I will be in Erice, Sicily,
this summer and they have a "funicular"
from Trapani up to the top of the mountain
where the poetry reading is. "I'm afraid of it,"
I tell my friend who can do physical
things with ease. "What if your grandson
wants to go on it," she asks.
"Oh," I say, "I'll risk it for him."
But the whole time I'll be worried
we'll slide off the mountain into the sea.

My American Grandson in Italy

My grandson takes a video of me with my cousins, as we sit
at a round table at my cousin Maria's house in Cilento.
Maria has once again gotten up early and spent hours making
pasticelle, which I love, and which reminds me of my mother.
We are all excited and we are gossiping and exchanging stories
about our grandparents, and Jackson captures us on video,
all of us talking at once, our voices crossing over one another,
our hands moving, our Cilentano dialect,
even my broken Italian, but most of all the way we use
our hands to talk. I am so happy in their company,
these women, these first cousins, who welcome me
into their circle as though I had grown up in Cilento,
instead of New Jersey, and I feel no distance between us,
love it when they hug me or touch my hand. In the video,
we are all smiling and laughing. How fortunate we are
to have these moments to hold in our memories,
so sweet and perfect, so Italian
that my American grandson thinks it's funny
to take a video of us chattering
and waving our hands.

Italian Summer

This summer in Italy, you helped me up steps,
let me hold your arm as we walked
the cobblestone streets of Italian hill towns.
I wanted to give you a gift of the Italy I love, grandson.
How easy it is to believe what we want to believe
about the way people see us,
what they feel.

For years, I held onto the image of you
at seven years old in your North Carolina house.
You walked past me in your family room,
backed up, looked at me with huge violet eyes.
"I love you, Grandma," you said.

Or the way you always grabbed your pillow
and overnight bag because you wanted to stay
with me at the hotel when I visited you,
so much sweetness always coming off you,
such an open, loving heart.

Now, you're 19 and we are in Italy together. We have
been here almost three weeks. I am happy
to walk with you, to watch you try new food.
At my favorite restaurant in Rome, we have dinner together
and you drink your glass of champagne and mine.
Suddenly, you turn to me and tell me everything
your mother and father say about me, all the things
that are wrong about me—too busy, too loud,
too enthusiastic—all the things I should have done,
and in the restaurant, where I will never be able to go again,
I start to cry.

We leave the restaurant and you take my arm.
But my throat clamps closed. I can't speak.
How foolish I feel for believing you loved me
as I have always loved you.

Now, each night, I pray for you to do well
in your classes, to be happy, to make friends.
I love you no less,
though whenever I think of you I am sad
for this loss, a cave that opens inside me
too deep and dark ever to fill.

In Sicily

My 19-year-old grandson gives me his arm, lugs me up
the steps of the bus, helps me up hills and mountains,
his eyes drinking in the beauty of Sicily, its exquisite
flowers, its elaborate churches, its ancient temples
that stand stark against the bright sky.

We sit in cafes together and order
an enormous lemon ice that is served
to us in one of those Sicilian lemons
three times the size of lemons we have at home.
Time slows in the hot afternoon
while we sit shaded by patio umbrellas
and almost purr like cats snoozing
through long afternoons.

When we get to Mt. Etna, my grandson climbs
to the top of the volcano, or as far up
as they'll allow people to go.
He loves the challenge of the climb,
carries a volcanic rock back to the cafe
where I wait for him. The guide tells us these rocks
are what make the Sicilian roses
so perfect and perfumed.

When we get home, I push some of these rocks
into the soil around my rose bushes
and watch them bloom,
as though I'd carried Sicily home with me,
the huge Sicilian sky, the mountains,
the people with their tables laden with food
and smiles of welcome,
this place so ancient and unchanging,
so alive with color and light,
whose music calls me back to it again and again,
as though it, and not New Jersey,
were home.

Artifacts

No artifacts remain from my parents' childhood.
They grew up in a small village on the side of a mountain
in southern Italy, came to America as young adults,
brought with them nothing
because they had nothing
except my mother's biancheria:
the linens her mother and grandmother stitched,
the towels she embroidered. She and her mother
packed the biancheria in a metal trunk and she brought
that with her on the ship when she took the journey
in steerage. My mother left school after third grade,
cooked each day for her family of nine, then walked
up the mountain to the fields they farmed.
She had no toys and she did not believe in them,
practical and no-nonsense as she was.
We got white cotton underwear for Christmas and birthdays.
No dolls. No toys. She did buy games—Monopoly,
dominoes and cards. She wanted us to play together
so that my brother and sister and I would remain friends
our entire lives. When my children were growing up,
I practically drowned them in toys, but I think now
those toys were really for that little girl who still lives
inside me, the one who wanted toys
but did not know how to ask,
the one who looked at her friend's toys with longing.
I wanted my children to have everything I didn't—
that suburban life, the private schools, long family vacations.
I think now that I gave them what I wanted, and perhaps,
not what they wanted at all.

The Lace Tablecloth and the Patterns of Memory

My mother came from Italy and she brought with her
a trunk full of linens she had embroidered or appliqued,
lace she had crocheted into tablecloths and dresser scarves.
My mother packed them in a large metal trunk
and each year added sheets she bought with pennies saved
from her 25 cents an hour job in the factories of Paterson.
I used the tablecloths and linens in all the years of our marriage
when we had company or on holidays, and after we'd eaten
together in my dining room, my mother would take them home
to wash and iron, and bring them back white and starched
and pristine. My mother died 22 years ago; my husband
in 2010. But today, I open the drawer
where I keep the lace tablecloths and linens, and see
my husband and me as a young couple, my husband handsome
with his high cheekbones and gray eyes, my mother, father,
and sister still alive and vibrant, our children and our nieces
and nephews all there. I see in the lace pattern
the pattern of our lives, the way it winds in and out,
connecting all who came before,
love and marriage and grief woven
into the threads, and know
that all the people I have loved are tucked away
carefully in my mind, so that I can lift them out
and remember and be comforted.

My Mother Held Me

Someone asks, "Did your mother ever hold you?"
I think of the times I sat in her kitchen and cried,
the way she'd put her arms around me, the way
she'd smooth the hair away from my face,
wipe away my tears.

When I was a child, she'd hold us in her lap
while she told Italian fairy tales or stories
about her parents in Italy, whom we'd never met.
My mother was tough, sturdy, practical.
She did not coddle us. Knew
we had to be sturdy in order to survive.
In her house, there were cookies and cake
she made from scratch, nothing store bought,
but my mother held us, even when
she was working so hard she didn't have time
to slow down. She held us with her fierce love,
her belly laugh, her flour-covered hands.

I tell my friend I spoke to my mother every day,
no matter where I was, no matter how
far away, her voice a chord, the connection
between us necessary and irreplaceable.
My friend, who calls her mother once a month or so
can't understand, but I say, "I'm Italian.
I talk to my daughter every day
as I talked to my mother. I'm Italian.
We live in each other's pockets."
Even now that my mother has been in her grave
for 25 years, I carry her voice with me;
often I find myself talking to her as though
she were still alive, as though I could really
hold her hand, and remember that when
I was a young mother I'd get annoyed at her
when she called me to berate me for letting

the children run barefoot in the house
or for not cleaning my house the way
she thought I should,
and now, so many years after she has died,
I'm sure she is in my car, in my kitchen with me,
sure she is still trying to protect me,
as she always did,
still ready to offer comfort
when I am most in need.

This Morning, I Want to Write a Hymn

This morning, I want to write a hymn
to the beauty hidden in the cracks
of inner city sidewalks,
the hardy flowers that push
themselves up through broken asphalt,
to the homeless men gathered
in the vacant lot, to the thrift store
with its second-hand refrigerators
and car seats lined up in front.

I want to write a hymn to all
these young women pushing
baby strollers up Broadway,
to the memory of my mother
and all her years working in the factory
on River Street, and later in the one off Main,
she, determined to keep going,
working hard because that is what
she knew to do.

I want to write a hymn to her leather purses
bought at garage sales,
to the five-and-ten-cent knickknacks
she bought with hoarded pennies,
trying to make a cold-water flat pretty,
to the energy that burned off her like a coal fire,
to the way she let me snuggle up to her
when I was young and skinny and always cold.

I want to write a hymn to all the women from my past,
those Italian women sitting under the grape arbor
in their black mourning dresses, telling stories
and gossiping, while the men played cards
at the oilcloth-covered table
and the children sat quietly, listening.

I want to write a hymn to these women
who taught me that nothing can break you,
that if they could survive,
anyone could.

What Is It About Morning Light?

This is a love song for Paterson,
the city where I was born and grew up,
the one I couldn't wait to escape, thinking
I could leave behind the skin
I was born in, the life of always making do.

Yet now, looking back over a distance
of more than 60 years, I want to praise the energy
of the city, praise the exuberance of the Great Falls,
the freedom of long summer days spent outside
in the vacant lots or the street, the games
we played, hide-and-seek, hopscotch, jacks,
the wild flowers, daisies and black-eyed Susans,
that filled the lots, as if some magic hand
scattered the seeds of the flowers
that delighted us.

This is a love song to this city that welcomed
so many immigrants and still does, so that now
instead of Irish or Italian, our neighborhood is full
of Syrians, Yugoslavians, Croatians, Armenians,
all their people pouring into the city, giving it new life,
new blood, weaving themselves in the fabric
of the city, working toward new lives for themselves
and their children, the pot of the city bubbling
with so much hope.

Dream Sequence

I imagine moving under green water
as though I could breathe without an air tank.

I am a silver fish and imagine goldfish gliding
past without noticing me,

and I, my body suddenly free of awkwardness,
move with such grace, I could be

a young girl again, lithe and slender,
as though I had been born to inhabit this world

like the sea creatures, my body shimmering
in the watery dark.

It's been a week

*...of looking upward, inward, below the surface
and back in time.* The New York Times, D3, May 5, 2013

This year has been a year like that for me,
you, already three years dead and crossed over
to that other place where I cannot touch you,
and I left behind looking upward to that place
where I imagine heaven is
and where I hope you can feel me missing you.
NASA announces its plans to bring a piece
of Mars back to earth. I'd like to imagine
I could bring back some memento of you.

I read about a 23-million-year-old insect
of a previously unknown species found in Europe,
so perfectly preserved in amber that each tiny digit
of the 1.8-inch-long animal is clearly visible,
all its soft tissue intact.

Sitting in my recliner now, in our family room
in the evenings, my legs elevated, my eyes fixed firmly
on the TV screen, where I watch British mysteries,
I suddenly have an image of myself preserved
in amber, tears on my cheeks,
my hand clutching the TV remote.

What would the scientists of the future make of me?
This chubby woman alone in her empty house,
half asleep in a chair that holds her
like a huge brown hand.
They would stare and stare,
but how could they know
all the grief and longing that pulsed
below the surface of her skin
and in the chambers of her heart.

CPSIA information can be obtained at www.ICGtesting.com
Printed in the USA
BVOW01s1630080716

454831BV00003B/3/P